Anonymous

Condition Management of Empacipated Refugees in 1863

Anonymous

Condition Management of Empacipated Refugees in 1863

ISBN/EAN: 9783337330880

Printed in Europe, USA, Canada, Australia, Japan

Cover: Foto ©Suzi / pixelio.de

More available books at **www.hansebooks.com**

PRELIMINARY REPORT

TOUCHING THE

Condition and Management of Emancipated Refugees;

MADE TO THE

SECRETARY OF WAR,

BY THE

AMERICAN FREEDMEN'S INQUIRY COMMISSION,

JUNE 30, 1863.

[PUBLICATION AUTHORIZED BY THE SECRETARY OF WAR.]

PRELIMINARY REPORT

TOUCHING THE CONDITION AND MANAGEMENT
OF EMANCIPATED REFUGEES;

MADE TO THE

SECRETARY OF WAR,

BY THE

AMERICAN FREEDMEN'S INQUIRY COMMISSION,

JUNE 30, 1863.

PRELIMINARY REPORT.

TO THE HON. E. M. STANTON,

Secretary of War:

Sir—The American Freedmen's Inquiry Commission have the honor to report (preliminarily) as follows:

SECTION I.

NEGROES AS REFUGEES.

(District of Columbia, Eastern Virginia and North Carolina.)

All the investigations and inquiries the Commission have made throughout the above sections of country, all the evidence they have there collected in connection with the character and condition of the negro population who, from all quarters, find refuge within our lines, tend to this, that these refugees need not be, except for a very brief period, any burden whatever on the government; but that, on the contrary, they may speedily become, under a system of supervision not difficult either to arrange or to conduct, provided the proper persons be employed, auxiliaries to the government in its prosecution of the war, to the full as efficient as if the same number of loyal whites had emigrated into the Northern States.

The evidence before the Commission establishes, beyond cavil, the fact that these refugees are, with rare exceptions, loyal men, putting faith in the government, looking to it for guidance and protection, willing to work for moderate wages if promptly paid, docile and easily managed, not given to quarrelling among themselves, of temperate habits, cheerful and uncomplaining under hard labor, whenever they are treated with justice and common humanity, and (in the Southern climate) able and willing, on the average, to work as long and as hard as white laborers, whether foreign or native born.

The circumstances which have thrown them, for a time, on the care of the government for support, are such as operate equally upon indigent whites arrested in their ordinary course of labor by the operations of the war, and it is a mistake to suppose that assistance has been needed or obtained exclusively by persons of color in consequence of such disturbance. In some places, the number of poor whites succored has been greater than that of poor blacks. In November last, Major-General Butler was feeding, in New Orleans, thirty-two thousand whites, seventeen thousand of whom were British-born subjects, and only ten thousand negroes; these last chiefly women and children, the able-bodied negro men being usually employed on abandoned plantations.*

Nor, where relief has been required by both whites and blacks, have the latter usually applied for or received, in proportion to numbers, nearly as much as the former. Mr. Vincent Colyer, appointed by General Burnside, at Newbern, N. C., Superintendent of the Poor, white and black, reports that while seven thousand five hundred colored persons and eighteen hundred white persons received relief through his instrumentality, the average proportion dealt out in each of the staple articles of food—as flour, beef, bacon, bread, &c.—was about as one for each colored person relieved to sixteen for each white person to whom such relief was granted.† At the time this occurred, work was offered to both blacks and whites; to the whites at the rate of $12 a month, and to the blacks at the rate of $8 a month.

Under any circumstances, and in all large societies, even during a normal and peaceful condition of things, there will be found a certain amount of vagrancy and a certain number of indigent poor, disabled or improvident, to whom it is a custom and a duty to extend relief. Beyond this, except as an expedient for the time being, the Commission believe that the refu-

* General Butler's letter to the President of date November 28, 1862, of which a copy was kindly furnished to the Commission.

† The exact figures are given in a report made by Mr. Colyer to the Commission.

gee freedmen need no charitable assistance. In the city of Washington, containing sixteen thousand free colored persons, these support their own poor without almshouse aid, and scarcely a beggar is found among them.*

The vices chiefly apparent in these refugees are such as appertain to their former social condition. Men who are allowed no property do not learn to respect the rights of property. Men who are subjected to despotic rule acquire the habit of shielding themselves from arbitrary punishment by subterfuges, or by a direct departure from the truth. In the case of women living under a system in which the conjugal relation is virtually set at naught, the natural result is that the instinct of chastity remains undeveloped or becomes obscured.

Thus, stealing is a common vice among these people, when temptation occurs. Thus, they have the habit of lying when they deem a lie necessary to please a white superior or a defence against blame or punishment: under other circumstances, they are as truthful as the average of uneducated white people. Thus, too, many colored women think it more disgraceful to be black than to be illegitimate; for it is especially in regard to white men that their ideas and habits as to this matter are perverted. A case came to the knowledge of the Commission, in which a mulatto girl deemed it beneath her to associate with her half sister, a black, and the daughter of her mother's husband, her own father being a white man. Such ideas, and the habits thereby engendered, render it highly important that freedmen's villages, particularly when they are chiefly inhabited by women and children, should be at a distance from any military encampment, and should be strictly guarded. And as there are no sentinels so strict as the negroes themselves, the Commission believe, for this and other reasons, that colored guards will be found the most suitable and efficient for such service; and they recommend that, in every case, they be substituted for whites.

The testimony of the more intelligent among the Superin-

---

* An intelligent lady, wife of a physician in Washington, who has interested herself about the colored population there, and seen much of them, deposed before the Commission : "I have known but two instances of beggary by colored people during my residence of ten years in this city. A few are supported by charity from their own churches."—*Testimony of Mrs. Daniel Breed.*

tendents is to the effect that the vices above referred to are not obstinately rooted, and that each one of them may be gradually eradicated by a proper appeal to the self-respect of the newly-made freedman, and by a strict recognition of his rights. He is found quite ready to copy whatever he believes are the rights and obligations of what he looks up to as the superior race; even if these prove a restraint upon the habits of license belonging to his former condition.

An officer on General Dix's staff, acting as provost judge at Fortress Monroe, related to the Commission, in graphic terms, with what earnestness and conscious pride of his new position a negro, sworn as witness for the first time in his life, stood up to take the oath and deliver his testimony.

As to the false ideas touching chastity above referred to, the Commission believe that these can be in a great measure corrected by bringing practically to the notice of the refugees, as soon as they come under the care of the Superintendent, the obligations of the married state in civilized life. Debarred, as slaves, from any legal union—often from any permanent connection—unable to contract a marriage that is not liable to be broken up at the will of a master—they usually regard it as a privilege appertaining to emancipation to be married "as white folks are." The Commission think that, while compulsion in regard to this matter should be avoided, a judicious Superintendent will, as a general rule, find no difficulty in inducing refugees, when bringing with them those whom they acknowledge to be their wives and children, to consent to a ceremony which, while it legitimizes these relations, imposes upon the husband and father the legal obligation to support his family. This obligation, and the duties connected with the family relation of civilized life, should be carefully explained to these people, and, while they remain under our care, should be strictly maintained among them. The evidence before the Commission proves that, with few exceptions, they show themselves prompt to acknowledge and ready to fulfil such obligations.

If, however, cases should occur in which a refugee proves refractory, and refuses to acknowledge as his wife, or to marry, the woman with whom he has been living, and who is the mother of his children, he should no longer be allowed to cohabit with her or to live with the children; but if the proof of his previous relationship to them be sufficient, he should be compelled to contribute to their support from his wages, in the same manner as if they were his family by legal marriage. All this is especially necessary in connection with a proper system of allotment from wages—of which hereafter.

Some further remarks on this subject, touching on the social and family relations in the slave society of South Carolina, will be found in another part of this Report.

Sufficient evidence is before the Commission that colored refugees in general place a high value both on education for their children and religious instruction for themselves. In Alexandria, and in various other places, it came to the knowledge of the Commission that one of the first acts of the negroes, when they found themselves free, was to establish schools at their own expense; and in every instance where schools and churches have been provided for them, they have shown lively gratitude and the greatest eagerness to avail themselves of such opportunities of improvement.

As a general rule, they are more zealously devotional than the white race; they have more resignation and more reliance on Divine Providence. They have, also, more superstitions. These, however, the Commission think, should not be harshly dealt with. It is of more importance sympathizingly to meet and encourage, in these untaught people, the religious sentiment which sways them, than to endeavor, in a spirit of proselytism, to replace their simple faith in the Divine goodness and protection by dogmas of a more elaborate and polemical character. Practically, as regards the Christian graces of kindness and humility, we have as much to learn from them as they from us.

It is desirable that, as soon as possible, their schools and their churches be supported, in whole or in part, by themselves.

Medical aid they need, in the outset, and it should be provided for them; but here, too, the principle of self-support should be introduced as soon as circumstances permit. Vaccination ought to be strictly attended to.

SECTION II.

NEGROES AS REFUGEES.

(South Carolina and Florida.)

What has been stated in the foregoing pages as to the refugees that have crossed our lines from Eastern Virginia and North Carolina, though true in the main, also, of South Carolina and Florida negroes, is to be received with some modification as regards the former slave population of these two last named States, especially South Carolina.

This is one of the States in which the system of negro slavery seems to have reached its furthest development, with the least modification from contact with external civilization. There it appears to have run out nearer to its logical consequences than in any other we have visited. There it has been darkening in its shades of inhumanity and moral degradation from year to year, exhibiting, more and more, increased cruelty, a more marked crushing out, in the case of the negro race, of the humanizing relations of civilized life, and a closer approach, in practice, to a monstrous maxim; the same which a Chief Justice of the Supreme Court, perverting history, alleges to have been the sentiment of the civilized world when the United States Constitution was adopted, and in the spirit of which he assumes (in virtue of such perversion) that Constitution to have been framed; namely, that " the negro has no rights which the white man is bound to respect."* The evidence before the Commission shows that, half a century ago, its phase was much milder than on the day when South Carolina seceded. It is the uniform testimony of all emancipated South Carolinian slaves above the age of sixty, that their youth was spent under a state of things which, compared to that of the last thirty years, was merciful and considerate. As a general rule, these old men are more bright and intelligent than the younger field hands; in many of whom a stolid, sullen despondency attests the stupefying influence of slave driving under its more recent phase.

The disintegration of the family relation is one of the most striking and most melancholy indications of this progress of bar-

---

* Dred Scott vs. John F. A. Sandford, December Term, 1856.—23 Howard, 407.

barism. The slave was not permitted to own a family name; instances occurred in which he was flogged for presuming to use one. He did not eat with his children or with their mother; "there was no time for that." In portions of this State, at least, a family breakfast or dinner table was a thing so little known among these people, that, ever since their enfranchisement, it has been very difficult to break them of the lifelong habit that each should clutch the dish containing his portion and skulk off into a corner, there to devour it in solitude. The entire day, until after sunset, was spent in the field; the night in huts of a single room, where all ages and both sexes herded promiscuously. Young girls of fifteen—some of an earlier age—became mothers, not only without marriage, but often without any pretence of fidelity to which even a slave could give that name. The Church, it is true, interposed her protest; but the master, save in exceptional cases, did not sustain it, tacitly sanctioning a state of morality under which ties of habitual affection could not assume a form dangerous or inconvenient to despotic rule.

The men, indeed, frequently asked from their masters the privilege of appropriating to themselves those of the other sex. Sometimes it was granted; sometimes, when the arrangement was deemed unprofitable, it was refused. Some cases there were in which a slaveholder, prompted by his own sense of morality or religion, or urged thereto by a pious wife, suffered these connections of his slaves to have the sanction of religious ceremony. But it is evident that to connect even with such a quasi-marriage the idea of sacredness or religious duty was inconsistent with that legal policy of the Slave States which forbade to render indissoluble among slaves a relation which to-morrow it might be for the interest of their owner to break up.

The maternal relation was often as little respected as the marital. On many plantations, where the system was most thoroughly carried out, pregnancy neither exempted from corporal punishment nor procured a diminution of the daily task; and it was a matter of occasional occurrence that the woman was overtaken by the pains of labor in the field, and the child born between the cotton rows. Humane masters, however, were wont to diminish the task as pregnancy advanced, and commonly gave three, occasionally four weeks' exemption from labor after childbirth. The mother was usually permitted to suckle her child during three months only; and the cases were rare in which relaxation from labor was allowed during that brief period. On the other hand, instances have occurred in which the more severe drove the negress into the field within forty-eight hours after she became a mother, there to toil until the day of the next birth.

A noble exception, among others, to such a system of inhumanity, gratefully testified to by the negroes who enjoyed it, was to be found on the plantation of ex-Governor Aiken, one of the largest and most influential planters in the State. His habitual clemency, it is said, gave umbrage to many of his neighbor planters, as endangering their authority under a severer rule.

Under such a slave system as this, where humanity is the exception, the iron enters deep into the soul. Popular songs are the expression of the inner life; and the negro songs of South Carolina are, with scarcely an exception, plaintive, despondent, and religious. When there mingles a tone of mournful exaltation, it has reference to the future glories of Zion, not to worldly hopes.

If to the above details touching slave life in this State we add the fact that, because of the unhealthy climate of the Sea Islands off the South Carolinian coast (chiefly due, it is said, to causes which may be removed), the least valuable and intelligent slaves were usually placed there; further, that being much isolated in small communities, these slaves frequently had children of whom the father and mother were near blood relatives, producing deterioration of the race, it can excite no surprise that the negroes of South Carolina, as a class, are inferior to those from more Northern States. An intelligent negro from a northern county of North Carolina, who had there learned the blacksmith's trade, and had been hired to work on a railroad in South Carolina, stated to the Commission that he never knew what slavery really was until he left his native State. While there, he was comparatively contented. Within a month after he reached South Carolina, he determined to risk his life in an attempt to escape.

Yet the negro of South Carolina may be reached, and, with rare exceptions, he may, in a comparatively brief period, be in a measure reformed by judicious management. A chief agency in effecting such reform is the regular payment of wages for work done. Captain Hooper, the acting Superintendent at Port Royal, under General Saxton, having charge of some seventeen thousand refugees, testifies as follows:

Question—"Do these persons work willingly for wages?"

Answer—"I never knew a case in which a colored man had reasonable security for getting wages—even moderate wages—that he was not ready to work."

Such cases, however, occur, as other witnesses testify; but the general rule is as Captain Hooper states it.

Mr. Frederick A. Eustis, son of General Eustis, who owned the plantation on Ladies' Island, and who has returned to cultivate that plantation by hired labor, while expressing the opinion that the new system of labor in South Carolina was too lenient, and that "the negro should have no appeal, except in cases of extreme cruelty on the part of the Superintendent," gave the following testimony as to the people now working on his own plantation:

"I never knew, during forty years of plantation life, so little sickness. Formerly, every man had a fever of some kind, and now the veriest old cripple, who did nothing under secesh rule, will row a boat three nights in succession to Edisto, or will pick up the corn about the corn house. There are twenty people whom I know who were considered worn out and too old to work under the slave system, who are now working cotton, as well as their two acres of provisions; and their crops look very well. I have an old woman who has taken six tasks (that is, an acre and a half) of cotton, and last year she would do nothing."

But the great school for giving character to the race, in this State and elsewhere, is military discipline. Colonel Higginson, commanding a colored regiment at Port Royal, was asked:

Question—"Do you think that, as preparation for the life of a citizen, the organization of negroes into military bodies is important?"

Answer—"I should say, of unspeakable value."

Judge Smith, Chairman of Tax Commissioners for the State of South Carolina, deposes:

Question—"What is your idea about enlisting negroes as soldiers?"

Answer—"It is the best school in the world. If you could have seen the men who now compose the colored regiments here as they were before, lounging about with a shuffling gait, looking sideways with suspicious manner, and could have contrasted their appearance then with their present bold, erect carriage and free bearing, I am sure you would agree with me. It makes men of them at once."

The Commission bear emphatic testimony, so far as their researches have yet extended, to the truth of these remarks. The negro has a strong sense of the obligation of law and of the stringency of any duty legally imposed upon him. The law, in the shape of military rule, takes for him the place of his master, with this difference—that he submits to it heartily and cheerfully, without any sense of degradation. The Commission believe that, of all present agencies for elevating the character of the colored race, for cultivating in them self-respect and self-reliance, military training, under judicious officers, who will treat them firmly and kindly, is at once the most prompt and the most efficacious. In this respect, the war, if the negro be employed by us as a soldier, becomes a blessing to him, cheaply bought at any price.

Under proper treatment, public opinion among these people sets in in favor of military duty. No difficulty is anticipated in procuring colored men to enlist, provided those now in the field shall be regularly paid, and provided the determination of the government to protect them in all the rights of the white soldier shall be clearly made known to them; especially if this latter determination shall be signified to them by the President in his own name. Our Chief Magistrate would probably be surprised to learn with what reverence, bordering on superstition, he is regarded by these poor people. Recently, at Beaufort, a gang of colored men, in the service of the Quartermaster, at work on the wharf, were discussing the qualifications of the President—his wonderful power, how he had dispersed their masters, and what he would undoubtedly do hereafter for the colored race—when an aged, white-headed negro—a "praise-man" (as the phrase is) amongst them—with all the solemnity and earnestness of an old prophet, broke forth: "What do you know 'bout Massa Linkum? Massa Linkum be ebrewhere. He walk de earth like de Lord."

As to reform in the matter of chastity and marriage, it requires time and patience to bring it about. Much more than half the cases of personal difficulty requiring intervention among the emancipated negroes in South Carolina have arisen out of infractions of the marital relation. In this respect, there is a marked difference between South Carolina and North Carolina. Yet, even in the former State, the old habits are speedily yielding to better teaching.

General Saxton deposed :

Question—" Were the women, under the slave system, taught chastity as a religious duty ? "

Answer—" No, sir. They were taught that they must have a child once a year."

Question—" Has your observation led you to believe that the refugees pay regard to the marriage ceremony ? "

Answer—" Yes, sir. Whenever it is solemnized, I think that they do."

It is here to be remarked that, in the cities, there appears to have been a nearer approach to recognized marriage and to conjugal fidelity than in the country, and that there the Church succeeded better in repressing juvenile incontinence.

As a general rule, however, the religion of the South Carolinian slave was emotional, and did not necessarily connect itself with the suppression of vicious habits, but rather with church observances. It produced, indeed, submission, humility, resignation, reliance on Providence, obedience to masters; but its effect in checking lying, thieving, incontinence, and similar offences, was feeble and uncertain. A slave has seldom any distinct moral perception that he ought to speak the truth, or to respect private property, in the case of a person he dislikes ; but these people are easily reached through their affections.

Whether because the race is not addicted to intemperance, or that they were here cut off from its temptation, drunkenness is an almost unknown vice. Captain Hooper testified :

" I never saw a negro drunk, and I heard of but one case, and that was of a man working on a vessel at Bay Point, who got whiskey on board."

There is no disposition in these people to go North. General Saxton offered them papers for that purpose, but no one availed himself of the offer. They are equally averse to the idea of emigrating to Africa. These feelings are universal among them. The local attachments of the negro are eminently strong, and the southern climate suits him far better than ours. If slavery be reëstablished in the insurrectionary States, the North will indeed be flooded with fugitives fleeing from bondage, and the fears of competition in labor sought to be excited in the minds of Northern workingmen will then have some plausible foundation. But if emancipation be carried out, the stream of negro emigration will be from the North to the South, not from the South to the Northern States. The only attraction which the North, with its winters of snow and ice, offers to the negro, is that it is free soil. Let the South once offer the same attraction, and the temptation of its genial climate, coupled with the fact that there the blacks almost equal the whites in number, will be irresistible. A few years will probably see half the free negro population now residing among us crossing Mason and Dixon's line to join the emancipated freedmen of the South.

The chief object of ambition among the refugees is to own property, especially to possess land, if it be only a few acres, in their own State. Colonel Higginson testified to his conviction that the effect of bounty land would be much greater on the colored than on the white soldier. They delight in the idea.

Working for wages, they soon get an idea of accumulating. Savings banks will be popular with them whenever their confidence is won.

The negro of Florida occupies an intermediate place between the slaves of North Carolina and those of South Carolina. He is more enterprising and more self-reliant than the latter. As a general rule, he enlists more willingly, and makes an excellent soldier. Many of them were employed as lumbermen, and in other vocations better calculated to call out their intelligence than the monotonous labor of the cotton field.

SECTION III.

NEGROES AS MILITARY LABORERS.

Even under the present faulty or imperfect system of management, the refugee negroes furnish to the government, in various localities, in the shape of military labor, the full equivalent of the rations and the wages which they and their wives and children receive. Major-General Dix expressed to the Commission his opinion that such was, at this time, the case within his military department, with the single exception, perhaps, of a few rations to dependent women and children on Craney Island.*

To the same effect is the evidence obtained from Brigadier-General Saxton, Military Governor of the Department of the South, having about eighteen thousand refugees under his care.

* Stated in a conference which the Commission had with General Dix at Fortress Monroe, May 9, 1863.

He testifies that, all things considered, they have been no expense to the government.*

So far, in all the localities visited by the Commission, the demand for able-bodied negroes as laborers in the military service has greatly exceeded the supply. In many cases, the supply has not met half the demand. During the time Mr. Vincent Colyer was Superintendent at Newbern, the standing requisition by Major-General Burnside for colored laborers was for five thousand; and at no time was Mr. Colyer able to furnish over two thousand. Major-General Dix informed the Commission that he had never been able to obtain colored laborers enough, and that he had, at the time the Commission visited him, an order from Washington for five hundred, which he had been unable to fill.

While military operations are continued, the services of the negro can be made effective, in the prosecution of the war, even as a laborer alone, to a much greater extent than he has been heretofore employed. An officer, now acting as Quartermaster in one of the divisions of the Army of the Potomac, expresses, in a letter to the Commission, the opinion that at this time more than ten thousand white soldiers are detailed from the ranks for duty in the Quartermaster's and Commissary Departments, on fatigue duty at the various headquarters, on pioneer service, &c.; and that on marches, where guards for the trains, parties for cutting roads, building bridges, and similar labor are required, the number is much greater. If there be included the labor on intrenchments and fortifications, on garrison duty, in ambulance corps, in hospitals, as guides and spies, &c., it will, the Commission believe, be found, that one-eighth might be added to the available strength of our armies by employing negroes in services other than actual warfare. If we estimate our armies at eight hundred thousand men, this would give one hundred thousand as the number of negroes who might be profitably employed in the military service, not estimating colored regiments. Nor do we hesitate in expressing the opinion, that the duties referred to would be better perform-

---

* Testimony of General Saxton, taken June, 1863. He says: "The fact is that the colored people here have been of no expense to the government. They have received a good many articles of clothing from charitable societies at the North; but the balance of credit, I think, is largely in favor of the negroes."

ed by them than by white men detailed from the ranks; for all experienced officers know how difficult it is to obtain labor from soldiers outside of the ordinary routine of their duties.

In connection with the subject of military labor by refugees, the Commission here state that a proposal recently laid before the President of the United States by the President of the Metropolitan Railroad was submitted to this Commission, inviting their opinion upon it. Though important, this is a matter of detail on which the Commission are not prepared, at this time, to express an opinion.

The organization of freedmen employed as military laborers into brigades, with badges around their hats, labelled "United States service"—the men marched regularly to and from work —has been found, in practice, to have an excellent effect. It tends to inspire them with self-reliance, and it affords them protection.

SECTION IV.

NEGROES AS SOLDIERS.

The policy of the government in organizing on a large scale colored regiments, has been so distinctly announced, and is now being so rapidly reduced to action, that the Commission need do no more than say, in regard to it, that all the evidence which has come before them bearing on the capacity of the negro as a soldier, including the observation, in South Carolina and elsewhere, of negro troops, has confirmed them in the conviction that if the government can, before the end of the present year, bring two hundred thousand or more colored troops into the field, to serve during the war, the result will be alike advantageous to the cause of the Union and to the race to which these troops belong. Docility, earnestness, the instinct of obedience, these are qualities of the highest value in a soldier, and these are characteristics, as a general rule, of the colored refugees who enter our lines.

Another point in which these troops, when brought under military rule, show to advantage, is in their neatness and care of their persons, uniforms, arms, and equipments, and in the police of their encampments. Moreover, they are generally skilful cooks and providers, and exhibit much resource in taking

care of themselves in camp. These qualities will be apparent
to any one who inspects the negro regiments under Brigadier
General Wylde in North Carolina, or under Colonel Higginson
at Beaufort, or under Colonel Montgomery in Florida.

The spiritual or religious sentiment also strongly characterizes the African race ; developed in somewhat rude phase, it is
true, among Southern slaves—especially rude in the cotton
States—but powerful, if appealed to by leaders who share it, as
an element of enthusiasm. If the officers of colored regiments
themselves feel, and impart, as they readily may, to their men
the feeling, that they are fighting in the cause of God and lib-
erty, there will be no portion of the army, the Commission believe, more to be relied on than negro regiments.* But with
these people, rather than with a more independent race, success
depends upon whether their leaders are in sympathy with them,
have gained their confidence, and can arouse their devotion.
For this reason, however important a judicious choice of officers
is in all cases, the Commission consider that more depends upon
this in the case of colored regiments than in that of white
troops. It is probable enough that colored regiments badly
officered would be more liable to give way than badly officered
regiments of the more self-reliant white race.

---

* This was written previously to the publication of Major-General Banks's official
report of the assault made upon Port Hudson on May 27, in which he bears the following testimony to the good conduct of the colored troops who formed part of the assault-
ing force :

" On the extreme right of our line I posted the First and Third Regiments of Negro troops. The First Regiment of Louisiana Engineers, composed exclusively of
colored men, excepting the officers, was also engaged in the operations of the day.
The position occupied by these troops was one of importance, and called for the utmost
steadiness and bravery in those to whom it was confided.

" It gives me pleasure to report that they answered every expectation. In many
respects, their conduct was heroic ; no troops could be more determined or more
daring. They made during the day three charges upon the batteries of the enemy,
suffering very heavy losses, and holding their position at nightfall with the other
troops on the right of our lines. The highest commendation is bestowed upon them
by all the officers in command on the right.

" Whatever doubt may have existed heretofore as to the efficiency of organizations
of this character, the history of this day proves conclusively to those who were in condition to observe the conduct of these regiments, that the government will find in this
class of troops effective supporters and defenders. The severe test to which they were
subjected, and the determined manner in which they encountered the enemy, leave
upon my mind no doubt of their ultimate success. They require only good officers,
commands of limited numbers, and careful discipline, to make them excellent soldiers."

Colonel Higginson testifies:

"I think they will depend more upon their officers than white troops, and be more influenced by their conduct. If their officers are intimidated, they will be: and if their officers stand their ground, so will they. If they lose their officers, the effect will be worse upon them than upon white troops; not because they are timid, but because they are less accustomed to entire self-reliance." * * * * "They criticize their officers very sharply. There is as much difference here in the standing of the various officers as in any white regiment."

Major General Butler expressed to the Commission, in this connection, an opinion which they believe to be correct. He said:—

"Negroes are gregarious in fright, and, in that particular, the opposite of the Yankees. If a crowd of Yankees gets frightened, it is 'every one for himself, and God for us all!' Now, the negroes have been accustomed to stand in a body against master and overseer. At a sudden alarm, they segregate—they run to each other."

In connection with the value of the negro as a soldier, the Commission earnestly invite your attention to the valuable assistance which our Generals in command may obtain in exploring the enemy's country and detecting his position and plans, by the organization of companies of colored guides in connection with each army corps. On this subject, the Commission herewith submit a separate Report, to which they pray reference.

If, as the Commission recommend, colored troops to the number of two hundred thousand be brought into the field, and negroes be employed in our armies in operations other than actual warfare to the extent of a hundred thousand more, we shall require the military services of three hundred thousand blacks. This number of able-bodied men represents a population of almost a million and a half, being one-half of all the colored people in the insurrectionary States. To reach this number there is needed, besides military successes, a strict enforcement of the orders issued by the government, that all colored refugees be treated with justice and humanity. By such treatment alone can their confidence be won, and strong inducement held out to others to join us. Upon such treatment depends, in a great measure, how large shall be the reënforcements to be obtained by our armies at the expense of the enemy. Until a million and a half of slaves shall have forsaken their masters, we shall not have the full military advantage which we ought to derive from this source. It is evident that it behooves us to hasten such a result, and otherwise to promote the disintegration of the slave labor system of the South, by every means in our power.

If the placing in the field, during the war, of two hundred thousand efficient black troops—a measure demanded by the exigencies of a contest which was commenced by the South —should ultimately prove to be one of the chief agencies to prevent the restoration of slavery in the insurrectionary States, such a condition of things would supply evidence that the very effort to perpetuate an abuse has been the means, under Providence, of effecting its eradication. The Slave States will have been doomed themselves to forge a weapon to destroy that system, for the existence and extension of which, taking up arms, they have deluged a continent with blood.

In connection with the probabilities of our obtaining the above number of colored troops, it is the duty of the Commission to report the fact that, in too many cases, not injustice only but robbery and other crimes have been committed against fugitives on first entering our lines. As an example: the Assistant Superintendent at Suffolk, Virginia, informed the Commission that instances had come to his knowledge of pickets who sometimes kept refugees until their masters came for them, and sometimes sent them back, pocketing the reward; the examples, however, of this offence were not numerous. He stated further, that, "in hundreds of cases," the refugees had been robbed by the pickets, chiefly of money, but occasionally of other articles. Valuable horses, too, and other property, were taken from them by the Quartermaster, without remuneration to the refugee who brought them in.

The robbery and kidnapping by pickets occurred in the above cases, as doubtless in others it does, in spite of the efforts of the Provost Marshal to prevent it.

The practical effect of such crimes, of which the report soon penetrates into rebeldom, is, as regards the military service, the same as if white Union soldiers were habitually robbed by these pickets, or were from time to time seized by them and delivered over as prisoners to the enemy. Until such outrages are effectually suppressed, it is unreasonable to expect that disaffected slaves should desert their masters in numbers, to incur the double risk of running the gauntlet, first through the enemy's pickets, and then through our own. And this the rather, inasmuch as, from the relations they have hitherto borne to white men, and from the manner in which they have been treated by them, they naturally suspect the good intentions of our race towards theirs.

The above seems to the Commission so grave in its consequences as to justify a general order on the subject by the War Department.

As regards horses, wagons, and similar property brought within our lines by fugitives, it is proper, of course, that it be taken by the Quartermaster when needed for the public service. But, in such cases, it should be paid for as other property taken from loyal men is paid for, either to the refugee, if he makes no demand on the government for support for himself or for his family, or to the freedmen's fund in the hands of the Superintendent, in cases in which the refugee or his family apply for rations or other governmental aid. The capture and carrying off of such property weakens the enemy, and we ought not to discourage the practice by depriving the captors of the legitimate reward for the risks they incur.

There is no legal reason why the Conscription law should not apply to fugitives from labor as it does to white citizens. We have already, probably, placed in the field, since the rebellion broke out, a million and a quarter of white soldiers—nearly a third of our adult population between the ages of eighteen and forty-five. The investigations of the Commission, however, lead them to believe that if men of the proper stamp are selected as negro Superintendents, these can and will procure the voluntary enlistment of a much larger proportion of able-bodied refugees than this. The more intelligent among these people not only feel that it is their duty to fight for their own freedom, but, by a proper appeal, many of them can be made to understand that only by proving their manhood as soldiers—only through a baptism of blood—can they bring about such a change in public opinion as will ensure for their race, from the present generation in this country, common respect and decent treatment in their social relations with whites.

In practice, it has been found that, by judicious treatment, it is not difficult to create among these people a state of public opinion such that every able-bodied man among them who refuses to enter the public service when required, is tabooed by the rest, and falls into general contempt as a mean, despicable fellow. This was especially the case at Newbern, as reported to the Commission by Mr. Vincent Colyer, formerly Superintendent there. And the Commission believe it may be relied on in almost every case in which the Superintendent has succeeded in awakening the sympathy and winning the confidence of those under his care.

In all cases, therefore, the Commission think that every expedient (short of bounties, which they do not recommend) should be employed to induce volunteering by freedmen, before resorting to conscription or other coercive measures. Such measures, though for a time they may fill the ranks, are calculated to arrest that exodus from rebeldom of freedmen there held as slaves upon which we must depend to keep up the supply of colored recruits.

The Commission understand it to be your policy that to all colored soldiers of the United States shall be extended the same protection as to other United States troops, when taken prisoners by the enemy, as well as under all other circumstances. They cannot too strongly express their conviction that such a policy is demanded alike by justice and expediency, and that pains should be taken to make it officially and widely known.

SECTION V.

CHARACTER OF ORGANIZATION PROPOSED.

The researches and investigations of the Commission have not yet been sufficiently extended and thorough to justify them in suggesting a definite system for the ultimate solution of one of the gravest social problems ever presented to a government. Certain measures, however, are, in the present emergency, evidently demanded, not merely from considerations of common humanity, to alleviate the sufferings caused to non-combatant laborers by the forced derangement of industry consequent upon military invasion, but also in virtue of the fact that a great and radical industrial and domestic change, every hour in progress, and ultimately involving the eradication of a labor system which has been the growth of more than two centuries, needs, for a time to which we cannot yet assign a definite limit, to be, to a certain extent, facilitated and directed by governmental assistance and control. The two labor-systems—namely, that of enforced slave labor and that of free compensated labor—are, in spirit and result, so thoroughly at variance that the change from the one to the other by four millions of people cannot safely be left undirected and uncared for, to work itself out, drifting on at haphazard, according to the chance shiftings of the current of daily events. The transition has not yet so far proceeded, nor have its effects so fully developed themselves as to supply reliable data whereupon to base a judgment as to the exact extent or duration of the guardianship which the new freedmen may require. The system of apprenticeship in the English West Indies appears to have worked badly, and was terminated before the time originally fixed by law; but the defect may have been, to a certain extent, in its details: as to all which the Commission hope hereafter to be able satisfactorily to report. The question remains open, whether, and how soon, the American freedman, with the dependence engendered by the slave system still clinging to him—and what is worse, weighted down in his efforts to rise by that prejudice which prompts men to despise whoever has long been their inferior—will be able peacefully to maintain his new rights, and to protect himself against undue ascendency and imposition from the white man. Coming into competition with another race—one among the most energetic in the world—for the first time in the history of our country, on something like equal terms, will he, if left to himself, be overborne and crushed? And if he should be, will he bear it as patiently in his capacity of freedman as he has borne it under subjection as a slave?

On one point the Commission are already agreed, namely, that a scheme of guardianship or protection for one race of men against another race inhabiting the same country cannot become a permanent institution. If the necessity for the constant operation of such a scheme could be proved, the proof would amount to this, that the two races cannot in perpetuity inhabit the same country at all; and that the one must ultimately give way to the other.

The Commission, therefore, adopt the opinion that all special governmental measures, particularly those involving continuous expenditure, whether for the relief of poor Southern whites or of poor refugee blacks, or for the guardianship of such refugees, should be more or less temporary in their character, and should be prepared and administered in that idea and intent.

In this view of the case, the Commission state, with satisfaction, that, in the course of their inquiries, they have found unmistakable indications that the negro slave of the South, though in some respects resembling a child from the dependence in which he has been trained and the unreasoning obedience which has been exacted from him, and therefore, in many cases, seeking and needing, for a season, encouragement and direction, is by no means devoid of practical sagacity in the common affairs of life, and usually learns, readily and quickly, to shift for himself. This, the Commission think, it is just and desirable that he should be led to do at as early a period as is practicable, without further reliance, for aid or guidance, on the government.

In this view, the Commission recommend that all "contraband camps" (as they are usually called) be regarded as places of reception and distribution only, and that the Superintendents be informed that it is the policy of the government not to continue the aggregation of these people in military villages a day longer than is necessary to dispose of them as military laborers or on plantations, or in other self-supporting situations. A temporary exception to this may be made in cases where it is found that women and children can contribute materially to their own support by washing or other service for troops in the neighborhood. But camp life for women and children has been found by experience to be demoralizing. In a general way, when abandoned plantations can be had, it will be found more expedient and more profitable to cultivate these, even though chiefly by women and children under eighteen years old, than to leave such persons dependent on mere village employment.

Upon the same principle, the working of plantations by government should be undertaken as a temporary expedient, rendered necessary during the period of transition. But as soon as there are found loyal and respectable owners or lessees of plantations who will hire the freedmen at fair wages, this is to be preferred; or when the freedmen themselves have saved a little to start upon, or when they evince ability to manage a small farm or market garden of their own, such spots may be temporarily assigned to them, at a moderate rent, on forfeited estates, until Congress, which can alone originate a public policy in regard to such lands, shall make, if it sees fit to make, some permanent arrangement touching this matter. Ultimately, when these lands come into market, the desirable result is, that the freedmen should become owners in fee of the farms or gardens they occupy.

To the Superintendent it must, in a measure, be left to select one or other of these plans, according to the varying circumstances in different places. When freedmen are hired, in the neighborhood of the Superintendent Station, by the owners or lessees of plantations or of manufactories, it should be made the duty of the Superintendent to keep an eye over them for the time being, so as to ascertain that they have fair treatment and prompt payment of wages earned.

When refugees are employed by government in the cultivation of plantations, the Commission are of opinion that it is cheaper and better to pay them wages than to supply them and their families with rations, promising them half the crop. The custom in many places has been to give full rations to adults, male or female, and half rations to children under ten years of age. Thus, a family consisting of a man and wife and four children, two over ten years old, are entitled to five rations; a larger amount of food than they actually need. The cost of these rations in General Dix's department is $14\frac{1}{4}$ cents each; consequently, such a family there costs the government, in rations alone, $21 75 per month. But a white farm laborer in that vicinity can be hired for $20 a month, he supporting himself and family. The freedman would have been entirely satisfied to be paid at the same rate and on the same conditions; while, under the ration system, though actually receiving from the government the equivalent of $1 75 per month more, he feels as if he were receiving no wages, but barely food; and has to go in rags unless private benevolence eke out a supply of clothing. Funds to pay these wages might be obtained from the "cotton fund" and from the sale of other personal property abandoned by the rebels, and could be repaid when the crops were disposed of.

If, in any location, it was found that refugee laborers on plantations receiving wages had no opportunity to purchase, on reasonable rates or within reasonable distance, such articles of food and clothing as they required, the remedy might be—

1. Either to sell them rations at cost, and trust to their purchasing clothing elsewhere—an imperfect mode of remedying the evil—

2. Or else, that encouragement should be given to the establishment, under proper restraints for a time, of stores for the accommodation of the freedmen. The Department Superintendent (hereafter to be spoken of) might be instructed to enter into correspondence with Freedmen's Relief Associations in New York, New England and elsewhere, and to suggest to them that, instead of sending clothing and other supplies for gratuitous distribution, they would more effectually and more economically attain their object by entrusting on loan to some honest, trustworthy young person, who had been trained to retail business, and upon whom they could depend for repayment, a few thousand dollars' worth of substantial food, dry goods, &c., such as are adapted to the wants of these freedmen, at moderate rates and of reliable quality. All persons establishing freedmen's stores might, on recommendation of the Superintendent, receive from the General commanding a pass and permit to sell, revocable at any time in case of misconduct.

The Port Royal Relief Committee of Philadelphia established such a store last year at Port Royal, which has been eminently useful and successful.

If these stores be multiplied, it may be the means of introducing a useful class of young and enterprising settlers into portions of country abandoned by slaveholders.

It is proper for the Commission here to say, that scarcely anything is more essential to the good government and improvement of these refugees, than that the wages they earn should be promptly and regularly paid. Nothing so encourages their influx from rebeldom as this. And it is most desirable that a freedman should learn, as speedily as possible, that emancipation means neither idleness nor gratuitous work, but fair labor for fair wages.

If additional argument in favor of such regularity of payment were needed, it is to be found in the fact, well known to those who have had experience with these people as laborers, that where they are regularly paid, a single threat suffices, in place of all other punishment, to check laziness and other delinquency; the threat, namely, of dismissal. But if the payment of wages be uncertain, or delayed for months, such a threat has no force; and the foreman has no hold over those whose work he directs. In every case in which complaints were made to the Commission of the inefficiency of freedmen's labor, they found, on inquiry, that wages had been withheld from these men for months. White laborers would not work at all under such circumstances.

In connection with this regular payment of wages, and also with the suggestion heretofore made, that refugees acknowledging wives and children should be legally married, the Commission recommend a system of allotment, under which each married laborer or soldier shall be required, at the time his pay is received, to cede a part of it, proportioned to the size of his family, for their support, in all cases where that family is left dependent on the Government. In cases where the freedman shall have provided a home and support for his own family, the amount to be allotted can properly be matter of recommendation only. Yet such recommendation will probably, in almost all cases, be as effectual as a positive requisition.

As the basis of a system of organization of freedmen—a first step, without which all subsequent steps will be attended with uncertainty and embarrassment—the Commission recommend a strict and comprehensive system of registration, to take effect as each refugee enters our lines. This should include not only a description of the person, so as to insure identification, if possible, throughout life, but also all the facts bearing upon his legal claim to freedom. It should be stated to each, at the time he gives in his name, that he must not alter it hereafter, as slaves, when changing owners, are in the habit of doing. He should be made to understand that *aliases* are not permitted among freemen.

The specific forms of allotment and registration recommended will be found in instructions to be given to the Department Superintendents, which, if this report meet the sanction of the Department, the Commission will immediately prepare.

The Commission believe it to be another important feature,

in a plan of organization for the care of refugees, that such
organization should be substantially separate from and (except
when military exigencies intervene) independent of the ordinary
military administration of the army ; it being understood, however, that the refugees, on first entering our lines, come in
charge of the Provost Marshal, who turns them over to the
proper Superintendent, and that every Superintendent shall be
required to meet, to the full extent of his ability, all requisitions
made upon him by the proper authorities for military laborers ;
payments or other supplies to refugees not in military service
to be directly through the Department Superintendents, who
should be required to give bond as army paymasters do, and
whose reports should be made directly to the Superintendent-
General of Freedmen.

The Commission, specially desirous to propose no scheme
which might endanger a conflict of authorities, have taken pains
to submit this feature of their plan to Generals commanding departments whenever they have had opportunity : as to General
Schenck at Baltimore, to General Dix at Fortress Monroe, to
General Viele at Norfolk, to General Peck at Suffolk, to General Hunter at Hilton Head, and to General Saxton at Beaufort.
Each of these officers, when such a separation was suggested,
approved it in unqualified terms ; usually adding that it would
be the greatest relief to themselves to be freed from all care and
responsibility in regard to refugees. One of these officers remarked that he had rarely found military abilities and the special qualifications needed to superintend freedmen united in the
same person, especially in subalterns.

SECTION VI.

DETAILS OF ORGANIZATION PROPOSED.

The Commission suggest a plan of provisional organization,
for the improvement, protection and employment of refugee
freedmen, extending, for the present, over those districts of
country only with the condition of which they have become
acquainted, chiefly by personal inspection of the various locations, in part by reliable reports and depositions—namely, the

District of Columbia, Eastern Virginia, North Carolina, South Carolina and Florida.

The Commission have endeavored to adapt their plan not only to the immediate wants under the present condition of things, but also to meet such additional occupancy by federal troops of the four States above named as is likely to occur during the present year, and until Congress shall have had opportunity to legislate on this subject.

The Commission propose—

1. That the above region of country constitute three freedmen's Superintendencies or Departments, the first comprising the District of Columbia and Eastern Virginia, the second extending over North Carolina, and the third embracing the States of South Carolina and Florida.

2. That there be appointed for each of these Superintendencies a Department Superintendent, with the pay and allowances of colonel of cavalry.

3. That there be appointed as many Resident Superintendents in each Department as there are important stations therein, with not less in each than from three to five thousand freedmen to care for; these Resident Superintendents to have the pay and allowances of captain of cavalry.

4. That where the number of freedmen at any station shall exceed seven or eight thousand, and it is the opinion of the Department Superintendent, expressed in writing, that an Assistant Superintendent is required, there be appointed such assistant, with the pay and allowances of lieutenant of cavalry.

In all cases, necessary transportation to be allowed to such Superintendents.

5. That there be appointed such clerks and foremen as may be necessary to carry out the details of this organization, with wages of from one to three dollars a day, graduated according to the character of their duties.

And, finally, that there be detailed, as Superintendent-General of Freedmen, an officer of suitable qualifications, not under the rank of a Brigadier-general, to whom and to his staff be assigned an office in the War Department; his staff officers acting as secretaries, and otherwise aiding him in his duties of supervision.

It will be seen that this organization presupposes three grades of Superintendents, besides a chief as central head, thus:

One Superintendent-General of Freedmen for the United States.

Department Superintendents—One for each Superintendency, comprising not less than a State.

Resident Superintendents—One for each Residency, with not less than three thousand freedmen to care for.

Assistant Superintendents—One to aid the Resident Superintendent when the number of freedmen within the Residency exceeds seven or eight thousand.

Together with the needful clerks and foremen.

The plan will not, the Commission believe, be deemed unnecessarily elaborate when the possibility is taken into account that the colored population, for whose supervision it is prepared, may reach the number of a million or a million and a half before the current year expires.

The Commission further propose that to the general officer detailed as Superintendent-General of Freedmen be committed, until Congress shall otherwise provide, the general supervision, throughout the United States, of the colored population emancipated by the President's Proclamation and by Acts of Congress; and the duty of seeing faithfully carried out the plan of organization which may be adopted.

That to this officer, as head of the organization, all reports of Department Superintendents, and all requisitions by them for money or other supplies, be addressed; and that it be his duty to lay these, with such remarks thereon as he may deem proper, before the Secretary of War.

That if, as the freedmen's Superintendencies shall increase in numbers and importance, the officer aforesaid shall be of opinion that it will be useful to call together, from time to time, the Department Superintendents to sit for a few days as a board for consultation and for comparison of mutual experiences, it shall be at his option so to do, and of such a board he shall be chairman.

That each Resident Superintendent shall report at least once a month to the proper Department Superintendent, who shall communicate said reports, with such remarks thereon and such recommendations in regard to any requisitions they may contain as to him may seem proper, to the Superintendent-General.

That each Assistant Superintendent report to the proper Resident Superintendent, who shall communicate such report, with his remarks thereon, if any he deem necessary, to the proper Department Superintendent.

A competent surgeon and hospital steward should be appointed for each Residency, and an assistant surgeon added when the number of refugees attached to the Residency requires it. It may be necessary at first to give these officers the pay and allowances of officers of the same rank in the army; but it is very desirable that, as soon as possible, the proper relation between physician and patient be, in a measure, at least, established, by causing these medical men to depend, in part, for support on those whom they attend.

The importance of enlightened instruction, educational and religious, to these uneducated people, cannot be over-estimated. It is pleasant to the Commission to be able to state their conviction, that the freedmen, in every district of country they have visited, eager to obtain for themselves, but especially for their children, those privileges of education which have hitherto been jealously withheld from them, may already be depended upon to support, in part, both teachers and pastors. The benevolent and religious societies of the North are aiding liberally in this good work; and the opinion of some of those who have taken a leading part in these philanthropic efforts (as expressed to the Commission) is, that, with the aid of the freedmen themselves, they will be able, for the present and until the number of refugee freedmen shall materially increase, to supply, in most cases, the necessary literary and religious instruction. If, in the organization of the various Superintendencies, this opinion should prove to be correct, it is well. But organized efforts of private benevolence are usually uncertain in their duration, and a greatly increased immigration of refugees may so augment the number of freedmen needing instruction, that the demand for school teaching and pastoral care will exceed the supply. In that case, it may be necessary, in certain locations, that Government, for the time being, detail a chaplain to take the religious charge of a Residency; and that it pay the salaries of the necessary teachers until the freedmen's schools become self-supporting.

As to these matters, it should be made the duty of the Department Superintendent specially to report.

Meanwhile, the Government should afford transportation to any religious or secular teachers who are duly accredited by respectable societies, and supported, in whole or in part, from the funds of such societies.

As a general rule, the refugees will probably sooner be able to pay their clergymen than to provide the requisite number of teachers for their children. The freedmen of Newbern have recently invited a private of the Forty-third Massachusetts Volunteers, named Edward Fitz, of the Methodist persuasion and having a license to preach, to become their pastor, at a salary of one thousand a year.

The organization proposed will be incomplete in those parts of the Superintendencies here spoken of in which the ordinary courts of justice are suspended, unless temporary provision be made for a magistracy through whose action these people may learn the important lesson that the obedience which, as slaves, they paid to the will of a master, must now be rendered by them, as freedmen, to established law—care being taken not to encourage them to become litigious. In this view, the Commission recommend that wherever, throughout the Superintendencies aforesaid, Justices of the Peace and Circuit and other Judges have ceased to hold their sessions, a Provost Judge, if he be not already appointed, should be. The lack of such an officer at Port Royal is very much felt.

They further recommend that the proper Department Superintendent be vested with authority to bring to conciliation and settlement all difficulties arising between freedmen, except where resort to a Provost Judge or other legal tribunal becomes necessary. Where a case of difficulty occurring between a freedman and a white man goes before a Provost Marshal or Provost Judge, or before any regularly established legal tribunal, it should be made the duty of the Department Superintendent so far to act as friend and adviser for the freedman as to see to it that his case is fairly presented and tried; and to this end, in important cases, where necessary, to employ legal counsel. In all these cases, the Department Superintendent should give such counsel and advice as shall tend to justice between the parties, acting in person when practicable; but, if necessary, he may be allowed to appoint the appropriate Resident Superintendent to act for him as deputy, during his absence, in the settlement of minor cases.

It should be specially recommended to the Department Superintendent, in the settlement of all personal difficulties between these people, to act as arbitrator rather than as formal judge; adopting the general principles governing courts of conciliation. And it is confidently believed by the Commission, that if he shall succeed in gaining the confidence of the freedmen under his charge, he will, with rare exceptions, be able amicably and satisfactorily to adjust such difficulties without further resort to law.

As to the mode of appointment of Superintendents and employees above proposed, the Commission suggests as follows:

That the Department Superintendents be appointed by the Secretary of War.

That the Resident Superintendents and Assistant Superintendents be nominated to the Superintendent-General by the respective Department Superintendents for confirmation or rejection.

That clerks, when needed at any freedmen's station, be nominated by the Resident Superintendent to the Department Superintendent for confirmation or rejection.

That Resident Superintendents may, with the concurrence of the Department Superintendents, appoint foremen when needed.

But that the number of Residencies in a Department, and also the number of Assistant Superintendents, be determined, after a report on the subject from the Department Superintendent to the Superintendent-General aforesaid, by that officer.

In the above recommendations as to the mode of appointing subordinate officers, the Commission are influenced by their conviction that it is a principle of great practical importance in administrative organizations, that upon all officers to whom subordinates are immediately responsible should be thrown, as far as prudence permits, the responsibility, by selection of such subordinates, of having about them only men of character and of proper qualifications. When a workman has choice of tools, he cannot throw the blame of bad workmanship upon them.

The Commission here desire to record their profound conviction that upon the judicious selection of Department Superintendents and of Superintendent-General of Freedmen will mainly depend the successful practical workings of the above sketched plan of organization. The African race, accustomed to shield itself by cunning and evasion, and by shirking of work, whenever it can be safely shirked, against the oppression which has been its lot for generations, is yet of genial nature, alive to gratitude, open to impressions of kindness, and more readily influenced and led by those who treat it well and gain its confidence than our race, or perhaps than any other. The wishes and recommendations of government, if they are not harshly enforced, but quietly communicated by those who understand and sympathize with the African nature, will be received and obeyed as commands in almost every instance. It is highly important, therefore, that those who have in charge the interests of these freedmen shall be men not only of administrative ability, but also of comprehensive benevolence and humanitarian views.

On the other hand, it is equally desirable that these refugees, as readily spoiled as children, should not be treated with weak and injurious indulgence. Even-handed justice, not special favor, is what they need. Mild firmness is the proper spirit in which to control them. They should find themselves treated, not as children of preference, fostered by charity, dependent for a living on government or on benevolent associations, but as men from whom, in their new character of freedmen, self-reliance and self-support are demanded.

Superintendents imbued with this spirit and the views here recommended will, if they possess a fair amount of executive talent, find little difficulty in managing refugee freedmen, and, with infrequent exceptions, will meet with no factious opposition on their part.

In first putting into operation this plan of management, it is recommended that the present Superintendents in the Departments referred to be either confirmed as Resident or Assistant Superintendents under the new organization, or at once relieved from duty.

SECTION VII.

GENERAL RESULTS.

The problem, in the solution of which the Commission has been called to aid, is of a mixed character. Together with obvious and imperative considerations of humanity, it involves great questions of Christian civilization and of statesmanship. But most urgent at the present moment are its relations with the national struggle in which we are engaged, and with the issue of that struggle for good or evil.

Proposing hereafter to embody in a more maturely considered Report the more complex and difficult inquiries of a general character above suggested, the Commission dismiss these for the present with a single brief remark.

The observations of the Commission in the sections of country visited by them, together with the evidence obtained from those having most experience among freedmen, justify the conclusion that the African race, as found among us, lacks no essential aptitude for civilization. In a general way, the negro yields willingly to its restraints, and enters upon its duties, not with alacrity only, but with evident pride and increase of self-respect. His personal rights as a freedman once recognized in law and assured in practice, there is little reason to doubt that he will become a useful member of the great industrial family of nations. Once released from the disabilities of bondage, he will somewhere find, and will maintain, his own appropriate social position.

The Commission revert to the question in its relation to the existing insurrection. Its importance, in that connection, can hardly be over-estimated. If the slaves of the South are loyal to the Union, the North will have itself alone to blame if the war is not speedily and triumphantly closed. Scarcely any other question, therefore, is more intimately connected with the future destiny, prosperous or decadent, of this nation.

But in point of fact, it admits of no reasonable doubt that the Southern slaves, as a body, do desire release from bondage, from forced and often excessive labor, from arbitrary and often inhuman punishment. Their masters have sought to inspire them with a dread of "Yankee Abolitionists;" but while doubtless assenting, as the habit of the slave is, to these denunciations of Northern emancipationists, all facts prove that these men, as a general rule, see through the flimsy pretence, and are willing to risk severe punishment, sometimes death itself, whenever they have good reason to hope that, in deserting their masters, they will find in us just and sincere friends, able and willing to put them in a condition in which they may enjoy the fruits of their own labor.

But we, by our policy towards these people, may encourage, or we may discourage, that hope. The point on which they are peculiarly sensitive, and chiefly need assurance, is as to the absolute and irrevocable certainty of their freedom. We cannot expect this untutored race to understand the abstract proposition, that a great nation, after having solemnly declared, through its Chief Magistrate, that three millions of its inhabitants shall be for ever free, cannot, without utter degradation in the eyes of the civilized world, repudiate that declaration and reconsign these millions to slavery. They must have more tangible proof of the reality and unchangeable character of their emancipation. They must feel themselves treated *as* freemen, before they can fully realize the fact that they are and will for ever remain such.

We, by our misconduct, may give color and force to the misrepresentations of slaveholders touching our ultimate intentions towards the negro race. We may cause doubts in the minds of this enslaved people whether, in flying from ills they know, they may not encounter worse ills by the change.

. Every aggression, every act of injustice, committed by a Northern man against unoffending fugitives from despotism, every insult offered by the base prejudice of our race to a colored man because of his African descent, is not only a breach of humanity, an offence against civilization, but it is also an act which gives aid and comfort to the enemy. The report of it goes abroad—penetrates into the enemy's country. So far as its influence there extends, the effect is to deter the slave from leaving his master—therefore to secure to that master a bread-producer; and, by the same act, to deprive the Union of a colored soldier, and compel the government, by conscription, to withdraw a laborer from a northern farm.

The practical effect, therefore, of abuse and injury to colored people, in these days, is not alone to disgrace the authors of such acts, but to compel conscription, and to strip the North, already scant of working hands, of the laborers and the artizans that remain to her. Thousands of fields owned by white men may remain untilled—thousands of hearths owned by white men may be made desolate—all as the direct result of the ill-treatment of the colored race.

Such a spirit is not treasonable in the usual sense of that term; yet its results are the same as those of treason itself. It becomes, therefore, in a military point of view, of the highest importance that all wanton acts of aggression by soldiers or civilians, whether against refugees or against free negroes heretofore settled in the North, should be promptly and resolutely repressed, and the penalties of the law, in every such case, rigorously enforced. A prudent regard for our own safety and welfare, if no higher motive prompt, demands the taking of such precaution.

We have imposed upon ourselves an additional obligation to see justice and humanity exercised towards these people, in accepting their services as soldiers. It would be a degree of baseness of which we hope our country is incapable, to treat with contumely the defenders of the Union, the men who shall have confronted death on the battle field, side by side with the bravest of our own race, in a struggle in which the stake is the existence in peace and in their integrity of these United States.

We are unjust to our enemies if we deny that this struggle has been a hard-fought one; contested bravely and with varying success. A people with an element of semi-barbarism in their society, giving birth to habits of violence and of lawless daring, are, in some respects, better prepared for war than one which stands on a higher plane of Christian civilization. Add to this, that our task is the more arduous, because, to quell the rebellion, we have had to become the invaders. Under these circumstances, can we overlook the fact that several hundred thousand able-bodied men, detached from the labor-ranks of the enemy and incorporated into the army of the North, may essentially influence the decision of the issue?

There is an additional reason why a considerable portion of the Union armies should be made up of persons of African descent. The transformation of the slave society of the South into free society, no longer properly a question, has become a necessity of our national existence. Reflecting men have already reached the conclusion, and the mass of our people are attaining to it day by day, that the sole condition of permanent peace on this continent is the eradication of negro slavery. But the history of the world furnishes no example of an enslaved race which won its freedom without exertion of its own. That the indiscriminate massacres of a servile insurrection have been spared us, as addition to the horrors of a civil war, is due, it would seem, rather to that absence of revenge and blood-thirstiness which characterizes this race, than to the lack either of courage or of any other quality that makes the hardy combatant; for these the negro appears, so far as we have tried him in civilized warfare, to possess.* And in such warfare is it fitting

---

* At the moment of writing this, the newspapers of the day arrive, containing the following private letter from an actor in the fight at Milliken's Bend, and an eye-witness of the desperate valor of the negro troops there engaged. It appeared originally in the Galena (Ill.) *Advertiser*, and bears the marks of truth and accuracy.

THE GREAT GALLANTRY OF THE NEGRO TROOPS AT MILLIKEN'S BEND.

We publish below a very interesting letter of Capt. M. M. Miller of this city, of the 9th Louisiana (colored) Regiment.

Capt. M. is a son of W. H. Miller, Esq., for many years a citizen of Galena. At the time of the breaking out of the Rebellion, he was a student in Yale College, and had nearly completed his course. He left his studies, however, and returned home, enlisted as a private in the celebrated Washburne Lead Mine Regiment, from whence he was taken and made Captain of a colored company. His statement can be relied on as literally true, and we venture to say the history of the world shows no more desperate fighting than that done by his company at Milliken's Bend. Every man but one in his company was either killed or wounded, and many of them in a hand-to-hand bayonet struggle.

MILLIKEN'S BEND, June 10th, 1868.

DEAR AUNT:—We were attacked here on June 7th, about 3 o'clock in the morning, by a brigade of Texas troops, about 2,500 in number. We had about 600 men to withstand them—500 of them negroes. I commanded Company I, 9th Louisiana. We went into the fight with 33 men. I had 16 killed and 11 badly wounded, 4 slightly. I was wounded slightly on the head, near the right eye, with a bayonet, and had a bayonet run through my right hand, near the forefinger; that will account for this miserable style of penmanship.

Our regiment had about 300 men in the fight. We had one Colonel wounded, four Captains wounded, two 1st and two 2d Lieutenants killed, five Lieutenants wounded, and three white Orderlies killed and one wounded in the hand and two fingers taken off. The list of killed and wounded officers comprises nearly all the officers present with the regiment—a majority of the rest being absent recruiting.

We had about 50 men killed in the regiment and 80 wounded; so you can judge of what part of the fight my company sustained. I never felt more grieved and sick at heart than when I saw how my brave soldiers had been slaughtered—one with six

that the African race seek its own social salvation. The negro must fight for emancipation if he is to be emancipated.

If, then, emancipation be the price of national unity and of peace, and if a people, to be emancipated, must draw the sword in their own cause, then is the future welfare of the white

wounds, all the rest with two or three, none less than two wounds. Two of my colored sergeants were killed, both brave, noble men; always prompt, vigilant, and ready for the fray. I never more wish to hear the expression, "The niggers won't fight." Come with me 100 yards from where I sit, and I can show you the wounds that cover the bodies of 16 as brave, loyal, and patriotic soldiers as ever drew bead on a Rebel.

The enemy charged us so close that we fought with our bayonets, hand to hand. I have six broken bayonets to show how bravely my men fought. The 23d Iowa joined my company on the right, and I declare truthfully that they had all fled before our regiment fell back, as we were all compelled to do.

Under command of Col. Page, I led the 9th and 11th Louisiana, when the rifle-pits were re-taken and held by our troops, our two regiments doing the work.

I narrowly escaped death once. A Rebel took deliberate aim at me with both barrels of his gun, and the bullets passed so close to me that the powder that remained on them burned my cheek. Three of my men who saw him aim and fire thought that he wounded me each fire. One of them was killed by my side, and he fell on me, covering my clothes with his blood, and before the Rebel could fire again, I blew his brains out with my gun.

It was a horrible fight, the worst I was ever engaged in—not even excepting Shiloh. The enemy cried, "No quarter!" but some of them were very glad to take it when made prisoners.

Col. Allen of the 17th Texas was killed in front of our regiment, and Brig.-Gen. Walker was wounded. We killed about 180 of the enemy. The gunboat *Choctaw* did good service shelling them. I stood on the breastworks after we took them, and gave the elevations and direction for the gunboat by pointing my sword, and they sent a shell right into their midst, which sent them in all directions. Three shells fell there, and 62 Rebels lay there when the fight was over.

My wound is not serious, but troublesome. What few men I have left seem to think much of me because I stood up with them in the fight. I can say for them that I never saw a braver company of men in my life.

Not one of them offered to leave his place until ordered to fall back; in fact, very few ever did fall back. I went down to the hospital, three miles, to-day, to see the wounded. Nine of them were there, two having died of their wounds. A boy I had cooking for me came and begged a gun when the Rebels were advancing, and took his place with the company, and when we re-took the breastworks, I found him badly wounded with one gunshot and two bayonet wounds. A new recruit I had issued a gun to the day before the fight was found dead, with a firm grasp on his gun, the bayonet of which was broken in three pieces. So they fought and died defending the cause that we revere. They met death coolly, bravely—not rashly did they expose themselves, but all were steady and obedient to orders.

So God has spared me again through many dangers. I cannot tell how it was I escaped.
Your affectionate nephew,

M. M. MILLER.

race in our country indissolubly connected with an act of justice, on our part, toward people of another race; then is it the sole condition under which we may expect—and, if history speak truth, the sole condition under which we shall attain—domestic tranquillity, that we shall give the negro an opportunity of working out, on those battle-fields that are to decide our own national destiny, *his* destiny, whether as slave or as freedman, at the same time.

The Commission have been instructed to report how colored freedmen " can be most usefully employed in the service of the government for the suppression of the rebellion." The above remarks may suffice as the record of their profound conviction, that no more effectual aid can be had in the speedy suppression of the rebellion and the restoration of permanent peace, than is to be obtained by inducing the hearty coöperation of these freedmen, and by giving full scope to their energies as military laborers and soldiers during the continuance of the war.

Beyond this, it remains for the Commission to bring to your notice a statement communicated to them by Major-General Butler, namely, that many of the Louisiana planters, while professing loyalty, "had agreed together not to make any provision, last autumn, for another crop of sugar, hoping thereby to throw upon us this winter an immense number of blacks, without employment, and without any means of support for the future—the planters themselves living on what they can make from the last crop."

To what extent this policy has been carried out, either in Louisiana or in other States, the Commission have not yet the means of judging. Up to the point at which able-bodied freedmen are needed, as laborers or soldiers in the army—say three hundred thousand or upwards—there can be, for the present season, no difficulty arising out of any such combination among disaffected planters. Even beyond that point, the evident remedy is, that any surplus be employed in plantation labor. Meanwhile, women and children under eighteen can be so employed; and the produce of their labor may be of great importance, in view of the possible scarcity of provisions next season throughout the South, consequent on the destruction and consumption incident to war, and the non-cultivation of many plantations, whether by express combination of planters or from other causes. .

It is here worthy of remark, that in receiving any given number of colored emigrants from the rebel States, a much larger proportion of field laborers is to be found than in the same number of white immigrants; the reason being that the women as well as the men—even girls of fifteen and upwards—are usually accustomed to plantation labor, and often, from force of habit, prefer it to any other. This is an important item in estimating the aid which may be derived from negro refugees.

Upon the whole, the Commission conclude that there is not the least risk that such refugees will flock to us more rapidly than they are needed and than they can be advantageously employed. The only question is, whether we shall be able to induce them to join us in such numbers and as speedily as is to be desired. It is in our own hands to hasten the time and increase the number, and it is doubtful whether, in the conduct of the war, there is a more important duty to perform.

All of which is respectfully submitted,

ROBERT DALE OWEN,
JAMES McKAYE,
SAMUEL G. HOWE,
Commissioners.

www.ingramcontent.com/pod-product-compliance
Lightning Source LLC
Chambersburg PA
CBHW021621290326
41931CB00047B/1336